10/03

John Quincy Adams

John Quincy Adams

Sean McCollum

AMERICA'S
6TH
PRESIDENT

Children's Press®
A Division of Scholastic Inc.
New York / Toronto / London / Auckland / Sydney
Mexico City / New Delhi / Hong Kong
Danbury, Connecticut

Library of Congress Cataloging-in-Publication Data

McCollum, Sean.
    John Quincy Adams / by Sean McCollum.
      p. cm. – (Encyclopedia of presidents. Second series)
    Summary: A biography of the sixth president of the United States, provid-
ing information on his childhood, education, family, political career, time as
president, and legacy.
Includes bibliographical references and index.
 ISBN 0-516-22867-6
 1. Adams, John Quincy, 1767–1848—Juvenile literature. 2. Presidents—
United States—Biography—Juvenile literature. [1. Adams, John Quincy,
1767–1848. 2. Presidents.] I. Title. II. Series.
E377 .M38 2003
973.5'5'092—dc21   200211124

CHILDREN'S PRESS and associated logos are trademarks and or registered
trademarks of Scholastic Library Publishing. SCHOLASTIC and associated
logos are trademarks and or registered trademarks of Scholastic Inc.
1 2 3 4 5 6 7 8 9 10 R 12 11 10 09 08 07 06 05 04 03

Contents

Chapter 1

A Standing Ovation

On February 13, 1847, a carriage delivered a frail John Quincy Adams to the Capitol building in Washington, D.C. After a three-month absence, he was returning to his seat in the House of Representatives following a stroke. In his 80th year, he knew he was nearing the end of his life and of his long career as a public servant, during which he served as sixth president of the United States. Yet in his own view his long life in government was more or less a failure.

Yes, he was the son of John Adams, who had helped forge a new country and served as second president. John Quincy himself had played a hand in many major events in the growth and development of the United States. Yet his unbending stands and grumpy behavior had gained him more political enemies than friends. In Congress, his fierce arguments against slavery had often been answered with rage,

Lithograph of a photograph John Quincy Adams posed for in the last year of his life.

scorn, and even death threats. "The best actions of my life make me nothing but enemies," he wrote in his diary.

John Quincy could not have been more surprised, then, by his welcome that day. His fellow congressmen—admirers and opponents alike—honored his return with a standing ovation.

Pedigree of a Patriot ——————————

Eight decades earlier, on July 11, 1767, John Quincy Adams was born during the early events of the American Revolution. "Johnny," as he was called, was the second child of John and Abigail Adams. The houses where Johnny and his father were born and where they lived for many years still stand in Quincy, a suburb south of Boston, Massachusetts.

Father John Adams, a pudgy, balding lawyer, was often away, traveling from town to town, representing his clients. Later he went to Philadelphia as a representative of Massachusetts to the Continental Congress. While he was there, seven-year-old Johnny sent him a letter. "I have been trying ever since you went away to learn to write you a letter. I shall make poor work of it, but . . . Mamma says . . . my duty to you may be expressed in poor writing as well as good. I hope I grow a better boy and that you will have no occasion to be ashamed of me when

John Quincy Adams was born in this house in 1767. It shares a yard with the house his father was born in 32 years earlier.

you return. . . ." For the rest of his life, John Quincy Adams judged himself strictly and sought to improve.

When he wrote that letter, Massachusetts and twelve other *colonies* along the Atlantic coast of North America were governed by Great Britain. The Adams family and all American colonists considered themselves British citizens. Great Britain was governing the colonies harshly, however, and the colonists were growing angry. They wanted less British interference in their lives.

The colonists were especially touchy about taxes—money the government raised from its citizens by placing extra charges on goods being bought or sold.

The British imposed steadily increasing taxes on many everyday goods, claiming the funds would be used to help defend the colonies against enemies. Many Americans felt that the British had no right to tax more and more, especially since Americans had no representatives to speak for them in *British Parliament*, the country's lawmaking body. "No taxation without representation!" they shouted.

Between 1765 and 1775, the largest anti-British protests occurred in Boston. The city of 15,000 people became a flash point for British-American tensions. Johnny's father and their relative Sam Adams were in the thick of the political storm. On April 19, 1775, British soldiers marched to villages outside of Boston to seize arms and ammunition from Americans. Massachusetts farmers and tradesmen were prepared to defend their armaments. Political disagreement erupted into war when the British soldiers and the colonists exchanged musket fire at Lexington and Concord.

Colonial leaders, including Johnny's father, quickly gathered in Philadelphia to plan their next steps. In June, John Adams rose in the Second Continental Congress to nominate George Washington as commander in chief of the ragtag colonial army.

Back in Massachusetts, Abigail Adams managed the farm and family, now grown to three sons and a daughter. Though absent, John Adams advised his wife about their children's education: "John [Quincy] has genius . . . Cultivate their minds, inspire their little hearts, raise their wishes. . . . weed out every meanness, make them great and manly. Teach them to scorn injustice, ingratitude, cowardice, and falshood [*sic*]. Let them revere nothing but religion, morality and liberty."

Throughout 1775, the war swirled around the Boston area. In the early morning of June 17, seven-year-old Johnny and his mother climbed a hill behind their farm in Braintree. The roar of cannon had awakened them. From the hilltop, they could see a battle raging around Bunker Hill and Breed's Hill on a finger of land on the far side of Boston, and the British burning of Charlestown.

John Quincy and his mother could see the smoke and hear the guns of this battle on Bunker Hill and Breed's Hill in Boston in 1775.

★ **APPRENTICE STATESMAN** ★

As a man, John Quincy remembered the fear and danger of the time: "For . . . twelve months my mother with her infant children dwelt, liable every hour of the day and of the night to be butchered in cold blood, or taken and carried into Boston as hostages. . . . I saw with my own eyes those fires, and heard [Great Britain's] thunders in the Battle of Bunker's Hill."

The Littlest Diplomat

We . . . the good People of these Colonies, solemnly Publish and Declare, That these United Colonies are . . . Free and Independent States . . . and that all political Connection between them and the State of Great-Britain, is and ought to be totally dissolved.

With these words, the Second Continental Congress officially declared the independence of the United States from Great Britain on July 4, 1776. But the war still raged, and leaders of the newborn nation knew they needed help if they were to succeed. Later that year, the Congress appointed John Adams one of three American commissioners to France to seek that country's aid. Adams believed that if a country as powerful as France threw its strength to the American side, Great Britain might be forced to give up the fight.

John Quincy, now ten years old, pleaded to join his father on the diplomatic mission. As sad as Abigail was to see her son leave, she knew it was a great

Parental Patriots

John Quincy Adams's father, John Adams (born 1735, died 1826), was one of the Founding Fathers of the United States—along with George Washington, Benjamin Franklin, Thomas Jefferson, and others. Besides being a fine lawyer, John Adams possessed a brilliant mind for government. Many of his ideas found voice in the Declaration of Independence and the U.S. Constitution.

John Adams married Abigail Smith in 1764. Abigail (born 1744, died 1818) was a spirited, patriotic woman who sometimes seemed dissatisfied with the quiet role women were then required to play. In 1776, she teased her husband about this when he was on the committee drafting the Declaration of Independence: "Remember the ladies," she wrote. "Remember all men would be tyrants if they could. If particular care and attention is not paid to the Ladies, we are determined to foment a rebelion [*sic*]."

Years later, John Quincy recalled another childhood scene—his mother melting down the family's pewter tableware to make bullets for the Continental Army during the war. "Do you wonder," he wrote, "that a boy of seven who witnessed this scene should be a patriot?"

John Quincy's parents, John and Abigail Adams, as they looked at about the time John Quincy was born.

opportunity for Johnny to gain knowledge and experience of the wider world—while keeping his father company.

After a fearful six-week voyage in early 1778, John Quincy's European education began. This was a rare experience for an American boy of the day, and one that would shape his life and career. While his father *negotiated* with French officials, Johnny attended a boarding school. There he studied not only Latin and French, but also dancing, fencing, music, and drawing. The schedule was de-

Slow Boat to Europe

Forget e-mail or jets—during John Quincy Adams's boyhood, even trains were still decades in the future. With no power but the wind, travel by sailing ship between North America and Europe was an adventure that might include seasickness, rats, lice, disease, pirates, and shipwreck. If passengers did have an appetite, they often had to cope with maggots in their food. In 1778, Johnny and his father's passage to France took six weeks. Early in the voyage, their frigate outran pursuing ships of the British navy. Then a four-day hurricane tossed them violently, and lightning killed a crewman.

Such long travel times made quick communication between the United States and Europe impossible. Important letters and news took weeks to cross the ocean, if they were not lost altogether.

☆ ★ ☆

John Quincy as a schoolboy in Paris.

manding—students were roused from bed at 6 A.M. and studies continued until

7:30 P.M.—but Johnny wrote, "I like [it] very well." His quick progress in French

even made his father jealous.

John and John Quincy returned to Massachusetts in 1779, but within months, John Adams was dispatched to France once again. This time he took two sons—John Quincy (now nearly twelve) and Charles (who was ten). When Adams's diplomatic business took him to Holland, the boys traveled along. John Quincy enrolled at the University of Leyden, but soon he was swept up in another adventure. In 1782, the American Congress asked Francis Dana, John Adams's secretary, to go to Russia to represent the United States there. Dana spoke little French, the language used in the Russian court of Catherine the Great. So Dana enlisted John Quincy as his interpreter and secretary. He was only 14 years old, but he was mature beyond his years and spoke French as well as he spoke English.

Dana's mission to Russia was a failure. Russian leaders refused to meet with him or to recognize the United States as a new nation. Yet John Quincy was hardly idle. During his travels through Germany, Russia, Sweden, and Denmark, he visited every bookstore he could find, studied German, read classic books, wrote letters, and filled his journal with notes and observations. A few years earlier he had begun a diary, which he kept regularly until his death. It was later published and still provides a lively account of his long and active life.

John Quincy rejoined his father in the Netherlands and traveled back to Paris with him. During the Adamses' second stay in Europe, the Revolutionary

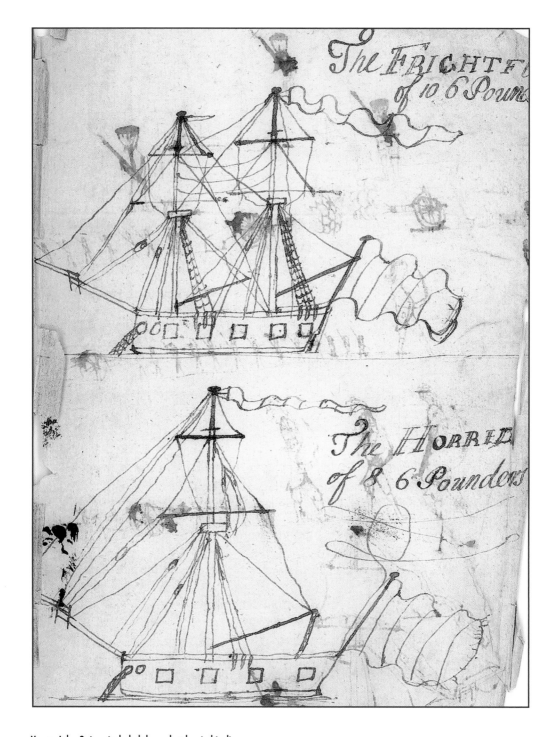

The FRIGHTF...
of 10 6 Poun...

The HORREE...
of 8 6 Pounders

Young John Quincy included these sketches in his diary.

War had come to an end. In September 1781, British general Cornwallis had been trapped in Yorktown, Virginia, by American and French troops and warships. He had surrendered his army to American commander George Washington. Now, in 1783, John Adams was going to Paris to help negotiate peace with Great Britain. John Quincy even helped copy some of the important documents. American and British negotiators signed the Treaty of Paris on September 3, 1783, officially ending the war. The British now recognized the independence of the American colonies.

In 1784, John Adams was named United States minister to Great Britain. Abigail and their daughter Nabby came to London to be reunited with John and Johnny. They had not seen Johnny for five years. When he appeared at their hotel, he was no longer the boy they remembered, but a 17-year-old young man. His father was proud of young John. In a letter to Abigail, he had described him as "the greatest traveler of his age, and . . . I think as promising and manly a youth as is in the world."

Home to a New Country ──────────

During his seven years in Europe, young Johnny rubbed shoulders with some of the great scholars and statesmen of the time. He had developed into a seasoned traveler and demonstrated a gift for languages. He had also adopted many European ways, including a large wardrobe with 65 pairs of stockings and numerous suits. He was not a flashy dresser, however—the suits were nearly all blue or black.

In 1785, he returned to the United States by himself, seeking a different kind of education in the land of his birth. "I have been such a wandering being these seven years," he wrote to an American cousin, "that I have never performed any regular course of studies, and am deficient in many subjects. I wish very much to have a degree at Harvard." His father had also studied at Harvard.

Friends and family warmly welcomed him as a minor celebrity. He loved dances, flirting with young ladies, and long discussions with his newfound friends. Yet he also found Americans rather rough and backward compared to his friends in the capitals of Europe. He sometimes offended people with his snobbish attitude and harsh opinions.

Harvard admitted Adams as a junior. He loved his studies but had little respect for many of his instructors. He particularly enjoyed math and the sciences, and praised algebra as being "as entertaining as it is useful." He learned to play the flute and refined his talents in writing and public speaking. Like other students, he also liked to sleep late, often dressed sloppily, and sometimes skipped classes when he caught spring fever. Still, he finished second out of fifty-one students in Harvard's 1787 graduating class. Now John Quincy faced a bigger challenge: What to do with his life?

John Quincy entered Harvard in 1785, where he became a top student.

Chapter 2

"What Am I to Do
in This World?"

The Sad Apprentice

After finishing college in 1787, John Quincy took up the study of law. Like all would-be lawyers in his day, he went to work for a successful lawyer, performing office duties, observing his mentor's methods and techniques, and studying law books in his spare time. Adams read law with Theophilus Parsons in Newburyport, Massachusetts. He soon realized that the legal studies held little joy for him. In his heart of hearts, he longed to be a writer and scholar, but he needed to earn a living. He also knew that becoming a lawyer was one way to begin a career in government and politics.

His discouragement turned into a dark depression, and he was haunted by a fear of failure. "The question, what am I to do in this world recurs to me very frequently;" he wrote shortly after starting the apprenticeship, "and never without causing great anxiety, and a depression of spirits. My prospects appear darker every day." His relatives watched in dismay as his misery took its toll on his health.

Love helped pull him out of his depression. In 1789, he met Mary Frazier and was smitten by the 16-year-old's beauty. In a poem for her he wrote:

The roses' colours in her cheeks to blend,

While Venus added, to complete the fair,

The eyes blue languish and the golden hair.

By 1790, John Quincy had completed his apprenticeship and moved to Boston to set up his own law office. He and Mary were very much in love and discussed marriage between themselves. When John Quincy's mother Abigail learned of the romance, however, she reminded him that at 23 and just starting his career, he did not have the income to support a wife and family. She also warned him that often youthful love does not last. John Quincy was still relying on his parents' financial support, and he respected their advice. After much discussion and hand-wringing, he and Mary broke off the relationship. Still, he remembered his first love tenderly even 50 years later.

Like most new ventures, John Quincy's law practice started slowly, and in truth he found his budding career quite boring. But then his pen caught the country's attention and set his fate in a brave new direction. Between 1791 and

1794, he wrote more than 20 essays that were published in American and European newspapers. In these articles he defended the new *federal* (national) system of government in the United States against powerful critics. When revolutionary France demanded that the United States support its war against Great Britain, President George Washington refused. John Quincy came to his defense, agreeing that the young country should avoid getting dragged into the conflict. John Quincy signed his articles with pen names (imaginary names used by authors) to avoid the possibility that he might embarrass his father, who was serving as vice president in Washington's government. Even so, many of his friends and supporters knew the author's real identity, including President Washington.

Impressed by John Quincy's writings and grateful for his support, Washington nominated his vice president's son to be minister to the Netherlands in 1794. When the U.S. Senate approved the nomination, John Quincy Adams, now 27, sailed for Europe. His long career in public service had begun.

The New Diplomat

Soon after John Quincy arrived in the Netherlands, the country was invaded by France. The French revolutionary government was now seeking to conquer the rest of Europe. It was not a good time to discuss the business of America with the

Dutch, but John Quincy sent valuable reports about the European war back to President Washington.

In 1795, another diplomatic assignment took him to London, where he soon realized he had much to learn. After being outsmarted by a more experienced British diplomat, he wrote to his father, "I have been accustomed all my life to plain dealing and candor, and am not sufficiently versed in the art of political swindling to be prepared for negotiating with a European minister of state. In other words . . . I have not the *experience* which the proper performance of the duty would require."

In London, Adams made another important discovery. He met lovely Louisa Catherine Johnson, daughter of an American businessman living in London. Although Louisa described John Quincy as a "sullen and silent suitor," he surprised her with a declaration of love. They were engaged in the spring of 1796, not long before Adams had to return to Holland. They were married in London on July 26, 1797.

Earlier in 1797, George Washington had retired and John Adams was sworn in as the second president. John Quincy believed that his father would end his diplomatic assignment to avoid being accused of nepotism—giving important positions to family members. George Washington helped persuade the new president to keep John Quincy. "Mr. [John Quincy] Adams is the most valuable public

Louisa Johnson and John Quincy Adams, at about the time of their marriage.

character we have abroad," Washington told John Quincy's father in a letter, "and . . . there remains no doubt in my mind that he will prove himself to be the ablest of our diplomatic corps."

With Washington's blessing, John Adams appointed John Quincy minister to Prussia (now a part of Germany), whose capital was Berlin. He represented the United States there for four years, throughout his father's presidency. In the election of 1800, John Adams was defeated for reelection by Thomas Jefferson. In 1801, before leaving office, Adams recalled his son from Berlin. He knew that Jefferson would be appointing his own supporters to political and diplomatic positions. In April, before John Quincy and Louisa left Berlin, Louisa gave birth to their first child, a son whom they named George Washington Adams. The couple were proud of their new son, but the moment was bittersweet. John Quincy was out of a job. After eight years abroad he sailed for home, again to an uncertain future.

The Senator from Massachusetts ——————

"I feel strong temptation . . . to plunge into political controversy," John Quincy wrote in his diary shortly after he returned to Massachusetts. He made a half-hearted effort to revive his law practice, but he was discouraged to learn that other young lawyers had gotten far ahead in their careers while he was serving overseas. Although John Quincy often scolded himself for vanity and pride, he was an ambitious man who strongly desired public praise and success.

In 1802, he won a seat in the Massachusetts state senate. Then in February 1803, the Massachusetts legislature chose him to complete the term of one of the state's U.S. senators, who had resigned. At the relatively young age of 35, John Quincy was suddenly Senator Adams.

Today U.S. politics and government are dominated by two parties—the Republicans and the Democrats. Political parties support candidates with money and organizational help, and debate important issues. The two dominant parties in 1802 were the Democratic-Republicans, led by Thomas Jefferson, and the Federalists, led by Alexander Hamilton. In general, the Democratic-Republicans favored limiting the power of the federal government and keeping many powers in the hands of the individual states. The Federalists supported a stronger federal government. John Quincy's father was the Federalist candidate for president in 1796 and 1800.

On the record, Adams was a Federalist. He had been chosen for the Senate by the strong Federalist party in Massachusetts. At the same time, he detested the idea of being a "party-man"—a politician who did whatever his party told him. Instead, John Quincy aspired to be a "man of my whole country." He tried to judge each issue on its own merits, then make a decision that he felt would most benefit the United States overall. This principle, though admirable, proved politically disastrous for Senator Adams.

In 1803, the United States negotiated the Louisiana Purchase, in which it would buy a huge territory west of the Mississippi River from France. When the Louisiana Purchase came to the Senate for approval, Federalists loudly opposed it. They argued that such a massive territory would prove impossible to govern. They also worried that new states set up in the region would be able to outvote the Federalist-controlled states in the Northeast.

Senator Adams saw things differently. He sided with the Jefferson administration and helped win approval for the Louisiana Purchase. He felt the deal would head off a future war with France, as well as prove a valuable step in the country's westward growth. His stand angered most Federalists, and some even viewed him as a traitor. Adams's independence continued to frustrate his Federalist colleagues in the years that followed.

In 1806–1807, Senator Adams again supported Jefferson when Congress passed the Non-Importation and Embargo Acts. Great Britain and France were at war while the United States remained neutral. Yet both sides were attacking American merchant ships at sea and refusing to allow the ships to trade with their enemy. The powerful British navy also took crew members from the ships, claiming

Thomas Jefferson was a friend of the Adams family when John Quincy was a boy. In 1800, Jefferson defeated John Quincy's father in a bitter presidential election. As a senator, John Quincy supported President Jefferson on the Louisiana Purchase.

The Louisiana Purchase

On December 20, 1803, the French tricolor flag was lowered in New Orleans, and the American stars and stripes rose in its place. The ceremony signaled the transfer of 828,000 square miles of North America from France to the United States. The deal, called the Louisiana Purchase, nearly doubled the territory of the United States. In the years to come the land in the Purchase would make up all or part of 13 states.

The Purchase was agreed to by Robert R. Livingston, the U.S. minister to France, and a young special envoy named James Monroe. They offered to buy the port of New Orleans at the mouth of the Mississippi River to keep it open for U.S. shipping. Instead, the French dictator Napoleon offered the entire Louisiana Territory, including New Orleans, for $15 million, or about four cents an acre. Napoleon needed money to carry on wars in Europe. He concluded that France had little future in competing with the United States on the continent of North America.

It was an offer the Americans could not refuse, and it marked a huge leap in the the country's westward expansion.

☆ ☆ ☆

that they were deserters. They *impressed* these men, forcing them to serve as crew on ships of war. Americans at home were infuriated by these actions.

President Jefferson was determined not to get dragged into war with Britain or France. Instead, he attempted a unique strategy. With the support of Congress, he *embargoed* (banned) U.S. ships and goods from leaving the United

★ "WHAT AM I TO DO IN THIS WORLD?" ★

States with goods for Britain or France—the country's two main trading partners. Both Great Britain and France relied heavily on U.S. *exports* (goods sold to another country), especially during times of war. Jefferson hoped that by blocking trade, he could keep American ships and sailors out of harm's way and that the embargo would force Great Britain and France to respect American shipping rights. For 14 months, most American ships floated at anchor. Without the ability to export goods, American merchants and farmers suffered.

The Embargo Act, prohibiting shipping of goods to Britain and France, ruined the shipping business in New England. Ships stood idle and grass grew on the wharves. Even though it hurt his section of the country, Adams supported the embargo.

Adams was the only Federalist in Congress who supported Jefferson's embargo. The powerful Federalists in Massachusetts were furious. The state's economy depended on shipping and trade with other countries. One Federalist newspaper editor called Adams unprincipled, "one of those amphibious politicians who lives on both land and water . . . but who finally settles down in the mud."

In June 1808, the leaders of Massachusetts took their revenge. They replaced Adams in the U.S. Senate. John Quincy wondered if his political career was over. In his journal he wrote, "Perhaps I have indulged the suggestions of my own judgment, and paid too little [attention] to that of other men."

Soon he would find another way to serve his country.

Chapter 3

Diplomacy in a Time of War ———————

After his rejection by the Federalists in 1808, Adams again found relief and success overseas. That fall, James Madison was elected president. In 1809, he appointed Adams to become the first U.S. minister to Russia, the giant country that stretched across eastern Europe and most of Asia. By now, John Quincy and Louisa had three sons. The youngest, Charles Francis, joined his mother and father in the Russian capital of St. Petersburg, where they arrived in October 1809. The two eldest boys, George and John, stayed behind with relatives in Massachusetts.

Adams enjoyed the life of a diplomat in St. Petersburg after the stress of Washington politics. During his daily six-mile walks, he sometimes bumped into Alexander I, the Russian czar, and they soon forged a valuable friendship. The two men would pause together and

St. Petersburg, then the capital of Russia, had been built on a grand scale by Czar Peter the Great in the 1700s. In St. Petersburg, Adams became acquainted with Czar Alexander I.

comment on the city's beauty, argue the value of long underwear in the cold Russian winters, and discuss world affairs. And there were plenty to discuss. John Quincy had a front-row seat during one of the most eventful periods in European and U.S. history.

By 1810, the forces of French emperor Napoleon had overrun most of Europe. Only two powers, Great Britain and Russia, blocked Napoleon's plan to bring all of Europe under his control. In June 1812, Napoleon marched 500,000 troops into Russia, driving the Russian army back to the old capital, Moscow. The French emperor could not defeat the Russian winter, however. Hundreds of miles from home and without supplies in a hostile country, the army began a long, disastrous retreat with Russian troops nipping at their heels. Freezing and starving, France's grand army was wiped out.

Meanwhile, in June 1812, as Napoleon invaded Russia, the United States declared war on Great Britain. The British had continued to board American merchant ships. In the Great Lakes region they were also providing support to Native Americans to fight settlers. At first the war went badly for the Americans, as British troops captured Fort Dearborn (at present-day Chicago) and Detroit. By 1813, after Napoleon's defeat in Russia, Britain could shift experienced troops to North America, raising further dangers. In 1814, a small British force captured Washington, D.C., and burned government buildings, including the Capitol and the Executive Mansion. Against the odds the Americans held out, defeating a British attack on Baltimore and turning back an invasion from Canada.

Napoleon's army suffered terribly from cold and hunger during their retreat from Moscow in 1812–1813. Only one soldier in ten survived.

Early in 1814, Adams received a letter from President Madison. Even though the war continued, Britain was tired of war and was ready to negotiate a peace. Madison wanted Adams to lead the American negotiating team. In August, the two sides met for the first time in Ghent, a city in present-day Belgium.

The negotiations were testy and difficult. At first, the British negotiators, encouraged by British military successes, demanded big concessions from the Americans—surrendering land, handing over valuable fishing territories, and giving up shipping rights. As the tide turned against the British forces, they gave up most of their demands. Slowly but surely, the two sides inched toward a peace agreement. On Christmas Eve 1814, the negotiators signed the Treaty of Ghent, officially ending the War of 1812.

Fast Facts

THE WAR OF 1812

Who: The United States against Great Britain and its Native American allies.

Why: The United States sought an end to British attacks on merchant ships and British support of Native Americans in the Great Lakes region.

Started: June 1812.

Ended: December 24, 1814, with the signing of the Treaty of Ghent. Because news of the treaty had not arrived, the Battle of New Orleans took place more than two weeks later, in January 1815.

Trivia: The 1814 British bombardment of Baltimore inspired Francis Scott Key to write the words of "The Star-spangled Banner," which later became the U.S. national anthem.

ports of Spain or of her Colonies, shall be admitted for the term of twelve years to the ports of Pensacola and S.t Augustine in the Floridas, without paying other or higher duties on their cargoes or of tonnage than will be paid by the vessels of the United States — During the said term no other Nation shall enjoy the same privileges within the ceded territories. The twelve years shall commence three months after the exchange of the Ratifications of this Treaty.

Art. 16.

The present Treaty shall be ratified in due form by the contracting parties, and the Ratifications shall be exchanged in six months from this time, or sooner if possible.

In witness whereof, we the Underwritten Plenipotentiaries of the United States of America and of His Catholic Majesty, have signed, by virtue of our powers, the present Treaty of Amity, Settlement and Limits, and have thereunto affixed our Seals respectively.

Done at Washington this twenty second day of February one thousand eight hundred and nineteen.

John Quincy Adams.

Luis de Onis

The signature page of the Treaty of Ghent shows John Quincy Adams's signature and red wax seal.

This great labor behind him, Adams now entered perhaps the happiest two years of his life. In May 1815, President Madison named him minister to Great Britain, a position John Quincy's father had held. Louisa and their youngest son joined him in London, and the two older boys arrived from the United States. (An infant daughter had died in Russia.) For the first time in six years, the family was reunited.

During this interlude, Adams spent many hours with his sons during long walks and study sessions. Besides his official duties, Adams also found time to read, browse bookstores, write poetry, and study the constellations beside his sons.

In late 1816, John Quincy received a letter from his father, long retired in Massachusetts. Father Adams urged his son to return home. "A man should be in his own country," John Adams wrote. "You are now approaching fifty years of age. In my opinion you must return to [the United States], or renounce it forever."

Soon afterward, John Quincy received orders to return home. James Monroe, who had helped negotiate the Louisiana Purchase, was elected president in 1816 to succeed James Madison. He called John Quincy Adams back to Washington to appoint him secretary of state.

John Quincy Adams when he was U.S. minister to Great Britain.

Secretary of State

The secretary of state oversees the relations of the United States with other countries. He or she also supervises the diplomats who discuss international problems and negotiate agreements and treaties. During his eight years as secretary of state, Adams had to use all his diplomatic experience to help steer the country through a stormy period.

In 1818, many boundaries of the United States were still in doubt. Both Spain and Great Britain had hopes of holding onto territory in North America. One of Adams's first successes was the Convention of 1818 with Great Britain. This treaty set a boundary between the United States and British Canada from Lake Superior to the Rocky Mountains. It also provided that the United States and Britain would both have rights in the vast Oregon Territory.

Settling the "Florida Question" the next year proved more challenging. In the 300 years since the explorations of Columbus, Spain had grown into a major colonial power in North and South America. But now its huge empire was coming apart at the seams. Mexico, Colombia, Chile, and Peru were all battling for independence from their Spanish masters.

Spain still held the Florida peninsula, but it could no longer control its border with the United States. The Seminole, Native Americans who lived in

Florida, were raiding and killing American settlers in Georgia. They also provided a safe haven for slaves who ran away from Georgia plantations. U.S. general Andrew Jackson was ordered to Georgia to defend against Seminole attacks and was given permission to pursue the Seminole into Florida if necessary. Jackson chased the raiders into Florida and then kept going. He captured two Spanish forts, and executed two British citizens who he said were helping the Seminole. Spanish and British officials were enraged.

Monroe felt Jackson was out of control and feared that the brash general could drag the country into war with Spain. John Quincy, alone among the president's advisers, defended Jackson. Jackson argued that if Florida stayed under Spanish control "there would be no security for the southern part of the United States." Any European power could land troops in Spanish Florida and threaten attacks on the southern United States. Adams agreed.

Spain saw the writing on the wall—sooner or later it would have to surrender Florida to the Americans. In February 1819, Adams negotiated a treaty that *ceded* (turned over) Florida to the United States. In return, the United States agreed to pay all of Spain's debts to Americans. Adams also persuaded Spain to clarify borders between Spanish and United States claims in the west. For the first time, the United States had clear claims to land that stretched all the way to the Pacific Ocean. For this reason, the agreement came to be known as the Transcontinental Treaty.

Spain was still hoping to crush the rebellions in Mexico and its South American colonies. Other European powers (which had colonies of their own in other parts of the world) might even offer to help Spain with the task. This would threaten serious trouble in the backyard of the United States.

To reduce the danger that European powers would intervene, President Monroe and Adams decided to make a public statement. On December 2, 1823, President Monroe included these words in his yearly message to Congress: "The American continents . . . are henceforth not to be considered as subjects for future colonization by any European powers. . . . [W]e should consider any attempt on their part to extend their [colonial] system to any portion of this hemisphere as dangerous to our peace and safety." In other words, the United States was warning Europe to keep its hands off North and South America.

This policy became known as the Monroe Doctrine, and it remains an important statement of American *foreign policy*. It contained many of John Quincy's ideas. The Monroe Doctrine had no immediate effect on world affairs, but it represented a new spirit in American policy, declaring that the United States would no longer be pushed around by the European powers.

President Monroe's cabinet discusses the Monroe Doctrine. Secretary of State Adams is at the left.

Becoming President ────────────

As James Monroe's second term came to an end, John Quincy Adams was well positioned to be elected president in his place. Presidents Jefferson, Madison, and Monroe had all served as secretary of state before becoming president.

The election of 1824 was no ordinary election, however. For 24 years the Democratic-Republicans had held the presidency. Their old opponents, the Federalists, had disappeared. Now there was only one major party, and its members were fighting tooth and nail for power. Several of them wanted to be president—so many that the election of 1824 was called "the Battle of the Giants." There were four main candidates. Democratic-Republicans in Congress nominated W. H. Crawford of Georgia. The legislature of Tennessee nominated war hero Andrew Jackson. Kentucky nominated former speaker of the House of Representatives, Henry Clay. Finally, Massachusetts and the New England states stood behind John Quincy Adams.

John Quincy was not a very good candidate. By his own reckoning, he was "reserved, cold, austere"—a grump. He did not like to promote himself, hoping that his long record of public service would speak for itself. Finally, he had a rare trait for a politician—he didn't like to talk. "I never knew how to make, to control, or to change [conversation]," he told his diary. "I am by nature a silent animal."

So why was he a top contender for president of the United States in 1824? What he lacked in charm, John Quincy Adams made up for in ability, stubbornness, and hard work. He worked effectively one-to-one with other leaders, as his long record of successful treaty negotiation and diplomacy shows. Friends and family also reported that when he was relaxed he could be witty and charming.

Adams was backed by powerful leaders, mainly from New England. Many, like Adams himself, were former Federalists who had joined the Democratic-Republicans in recent years. They relied on him to represent the political and economic interests of their region. His wife Louisa also contributed to his success. She disliked political life, but she displayed the social graces that John Quincy lacked. During the 1824 campaign, she tirelessly visited the families of key political leaders, and hosted receptions and dinners.

The presidential campaign was nastier than any since 1800, when John Quincy's father lost to Thomas Jefferson. John Quincy's opponents charged him with not being "American" enough because he had lived for so many years in Europe and married a British-born wife. They also charged that he was arrogant and hardhearted.

For the first time, states reported the popular vote for each candidate. Andrew Jackson, who promised to reform the federal government, received more than 150,000 votes. Adams finished second with 110,000. Crawford and Clay each received fewer than 50,000. According to the Constitution, the president is actually elected by members of the electoral college, who are chosen by each state. In the electoral college Jackson had 99 votes, Adams 84, Crawford 41, and Clay 37. Jackson did not receive the *majority* of electoral college votes—half the total plus one. In this case, the Constitution provides that the choice of the president should be made by the House of Representatives.

On February 9, 1825, each of 24 state delegations in the House had one vote for president. The next president needed at least 13 of these 24 votes. As the

Action Jackson

Andrew Jackson (born 1767, died 1845) was a true American-style hero, a bold, brash, romantic underdog. Born in North Carolina, he fought in the American Revolution at 13 and was orphaned soon afterward. He became a lawyer and moved west to Tennessee, then a "Wild West" territory, where he became a judge and a gentleman farmer. He gained his fame, however, as a military leader against Native Americans in the South and against the British at New Orleans. In many ways, he was the opposite of educated, disciplined, and sometimes snobbish John Quincy Adams.

Jackson's willingness to thumb his nose at authority won him the undying admiration of many ordinary Americans, especially in the South and West. "Old Hickory"—the nickname he earned for his tough, unbending leadership—was the people's favorite to lead the country.

☆☆☆

When the House of Representatives decided the 1824 presidential election, Henry Clay threw his support to Adams, allowing Adams to be elected. Andrew Jackson had won more popular and electoral votes.

fourth finisher in the electoral college, Henry Clay was eliminated from the voting. He asked congressmen who supported him to shift their votes to Adams. When the votes were in, Adams had 13, Jackson 7, and Crawford 4. So John Quincy Adams followed in his father's footsteps, becoming the sixth president of the United States. "May the blessing of God rest upon the event of this day!" he wrote upon hearing the news.

Soon his victory was clouded by scandal. Two days after the House vote, Adams named his former foe Henry Clay to be his secretary of state. Jackson and his supporters were astounded. Jackson announced that he had lost the presidency because of a "corrupt bargain" between Adams and Clay—the appointment as secretary of state in return for Clay's electoral votes. Adams and Clay denied any such bargain, but their enemies never believed them. After losing to Adams, Andrew Jackson began running almost immediately to win the presidency in the election of 1828.

Chapter 4

A Bad Start

John Quincy Adams was 57 when he took the oath as president of the United States on March 4, 1825. He stood five feet seven inches tall, with a medium build and a pudgy middle. White hair fringed his bald head and sideburns angled along his jaw. He had dark eyes and a pointy nose set in a stern schoolmaster's face.

In his inaugural address, John Quincy tried to deliver a message of optimism—and in 1825 there was plenty for Americans to be optimistic about. He reminded his audience that since the Constitution went into effect in 1790, the country had grown from 4 million to 12 million people. The territory of the United States, once "bounded by the Mississippi [River]" had been "extended from sea to sea." The country was at peace with all the European powers. The United States was enjoying the most peaceful and prosperous period in its 36-year history.

Adams also recognized that he had won a disputed election, which many still felt belonged to Andrew Jackson. Near the end of his speech, he asked for Americans' patience, understanding, and help as he started his difficult job. In the world of 1820s politics, he might as well have been shouting for help in a hurricane. His political enemies knew the new president was in a weak position because of the controversial election. Within weeks, they began to plot against his proposals. That June, President Adams experienced a sign of things to come—he nearly drowned while swimming in the Potomac River.

The Skinny-dipping President

As president, John Quincy Adams kept a daily routine of exercise. He tried to walk at least four miles a day, timing himself to see how fast he could complete the route. In summer, he switched to swimming, leaving his clothes beneath an oak tree and skinny-dipping in the Potomac not far from where the Washington Monument stands today.

On a June day in 1825, the president and his servant Antoine Guista found a "small canoe" tied to the bank. John Quincy proposed paddling the craft across the river, then swimming back. But halfway across, the old boat filled with water and the two men jumped out. The president was still dressed. He wrote in his diary, "My principal difficulty was in the loose sleeves of my shirt, which filled with water and hung like two fifty-six pound weights upon my arms. By the mercy of God our lives were spared."

☆☆☆

Soon after Adams's inauguration, he and Louisa arranged a reception for his opponent Andrew Jackson (standing to the left of Louisa). Jackson remained determined to defeat Adams in the next election.

If John Quincy had been a more flexible leader he might have realized that many lawmakers and other Americans were unwilling to follow where he wanted to lead. A more flexible leader might have listened carefully to what these people had to say and adjusted his goals. But John Quincy was not flexible and he did not like to take advice. He was an idealist with clear, strict ideas of right and wrong. He was sure he knew what was best for the country. His "I-know-better" attitude made enemies.

The Treaty of Indian Springs soon showed the flimsiness of President Adams's authority. In Georgia, most Creek Indians and their leading chiefs were against selling and leaving their land. But in February 1825, two federal commissioners bribed some lesser chiefs to sign this treaty giving Creek land to the state, opening it to white settlers and land dealers.

These shady dealings with the Creek bothered President Adams. He wanted to replace the treaty with an agreement fairer to the Creek, but Georgia's white leaders rejected federal involvement. When the president proposed sending federal soldiers to enforce a new treaty, Georgia's governor George Troup threatened to shoot them. "Georgia is sovereign [self-governing] on her own soil," Troup wrote President Adams. In other words, Georgia felt what it did inside its borders was its business, and the federal government in Washington had no right to get involved. President Adams was forced to back down, and the Creek were later driven from their lands.

This conflict between state and national government highlights big questions in American history: How much power should individual states have to do what they want? How much power should the national government have to interfere with what the states do? President Adams favored more federal power, and he learned the hard way that many Americans did not agree with his view.

Against the Tide

John Quincy Adams was a nationalist. He believed in one nation, its people working together for the good of their shared country. He believed a strong national government was the best means to speed the country's development and progress.

On December 6, 1825, President Adams outlined his vision in a speech to the Congress. He proposed building a national university to educate young Americans. He outlined plans for constructing a national system of roads and canals so that people and goods could be transported more easily. He recommended funding exploration and scientific research. He even proposed building a national astronomical observatory to study the stars and planets, as several European countries had done.

A portrait of John Quincy Adams painted during his presidency.

Today, none of these ideas seems extreme. Cars travel from coast to coast on a national highway system built with federal funds, and the government later spent huge amounts on astronomical study and the space program. But in 1825, President Adams's farsighted schemes were met with mockery. He did not help his cause when he suggested that members of Congress—the very men whose help he needed—were lazy and slow to take action.

His biggest blunder was thinking that Americans wanted a stronger national government to make their country better. Historically, Americans have distrusted a powerful central government. In addition, in Adams's day many U.S. citizens felt more loyalty toward their state than to their country. Someone from Virginia was more likely to take pride in saying "I'm a Virginian" than in saying "I'm an American." Naturally, people were more concerned about personal and local needs than about national projects and goals.

President Adams's proposals flew in the face of these feelings and beliefs. His critics rightfully argued that he was out of touch with what most Americans wanted. In the months that followed, his enemies attacked and defeated every proposal and plan mentioned in this speech. They even sarcastically accused him of being a "monarchist"—wanting to be a king. These charges stung President Adams to his bones.

The States During the Presidency of John Quincy Adams

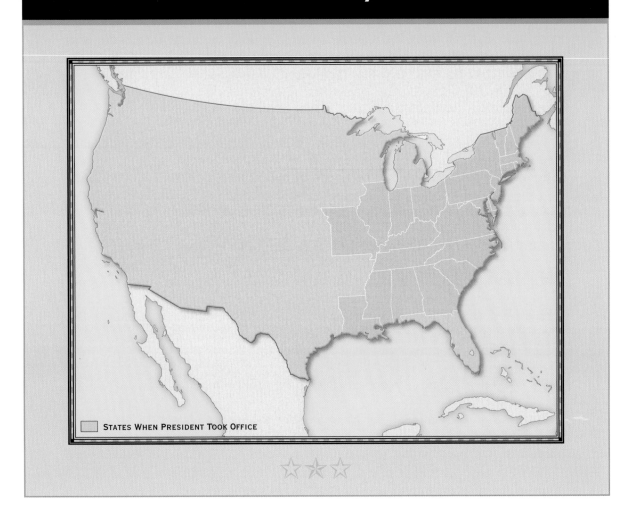

STATES WHEN PRESIDENT TOOK OFFICE

Whatever pride and happiness John Quincy felt in gaining the presidency soon faded. He tried to keep a regular schedule, but found himself dogged constantly by visitors. Many gained appointments with him to ask for a government job. In his diary he described one typical day: "[F]ive-and-twenty visitors, or more, from ten of the morning till five in the afternoon, leave me not a moment of leisure for reflection or for writing. By the time evening approaches, my strength and spirits are both exhausted."

One day, though, the open-door policy helped take care of a painful problem. A curious out-of-town dentist dropped by the White House just to get a glimpse of the president. Learning the visitor's profession, President Adams complained of a rotten tooth. The dentist pulled it on the spot and cleaned the president's teeth, as well.

The Terrible Tariff ——————————

As his four-year term dragged on, John Quincy found a few pleasant distractions. He added horseback riding to his fitness routine. He strolled the White House gardens and took particular pleasure in the growth of seedling trees that he had planted. In addition, his first grandchild, named Mary Louisa, was born in the White House.

At the same time, personal grief was added to his presidential woes. His father, John Adams, died on July 4, 1826. (Mother Abigail had died in 1818.) His wife Louisa became depressed and sick. In addition, the personal problems of his two older sons were growing increasingly troublesome. Louisa noticed that her husband had lost so much weight his clothes hung loosely on him, while a visiting niece described John Quincy as "a man harassed to death with care."

By the election year of 1828, President Adams's chances for reelection were fading fast. Then a final act of Congress—the Tariff of Abominations—put the last nail in his administration's coffin. Adams's enemies specifically designed this bill to humiliate him and help elect Andrew Jackson to replace him.

A *tariff* is a tax placed on imports—goods and products brought into a country. Adjusting tariffs can have a big effect on business by raising or dropping prices. Anti-Adams lawmakers wrote the Tariff of Abominations so that if the president approved the law, it would harm business in southern states. If he *vetoed* (rejected) it, then New England and Western businesses would suffer. Either way, President Adams would anger a big section of American voters.

Reluctantly, President Adams signed the bill, and southerners raised a howl. He tried to lay the blame on Congress, but the damage was done. Whatever support for reelection he might have found in the South was gone.

John Quincy Adams adored his wife, Louisa, though their personalities were very different. While he was often thin-skinned and demanding, she could be charming and playful. Shortly after marrying Louisa, John Quincy wrote his mother: "I assure you that I find [Louisa] every day more deserving of all my affection." And he wrote later that their marriage was the best event in his life.

Louisa was born in Great Britain to an American businessman and his British wife. She grew into a sophisticated young lady, educated in courtly manners, foreign languages, and music—she possessed a lovely voice, and played both the harp and the pianoforte. She also enjoyed writing poetry and short plays, and she loved chocolate, which left her with few teeth in later years.

Louisa Adams was an accomplished musician and also wrote poetry.

Her husband's election to president proved a sore trial for lighthearted Louisa. It "put me in a prison," she wrote. She hated the back-stabbing nature of Washington society and politics. She believed that politics brought out her husband's worst traits—bitterness, temper, and anxiety. She also disliked the White House. "There is something in this great unsocial house which depresses my spirits . . . and makes it impossible for me to feel at home . . ." she told son George.

In sickness and depression, she hid herself away in the White House for much of her time as first lady.

The 1828 presidential race between Adams and Jackson proved predictably nasty. Jackson supporters reminded voters of the supposed "corrupt bargain" between Adams and Henry Clay. They accused John Quincy of selfishly buying a billiards table for his own amusement at the White House. At the same time, Adams supporters unfairly charged Jackson with adultery.

Wherever Jackson went, citizens presented him with speeches and written messages declaring their support for him.

(Born 1782, Died 1850)

South Carolina's John C. Calhoun was a life-long public servant in the federal government— first as a congressman, then in turn as secretary of war, vice president, senator, secretary of state, and senator again. Calhoun had the support of both Adams and Andrew Jackson for vice president in 1824. After serving as Adams's vice president, he was elected again in 1828, and served in the Jackson administration until 1832.

Calhoun was at the center of many of the major issues that faced the government from his election to the House in 1811 to his final years in the Senate. He began as a supporter of Henry Clay's National System, but later became a strong spokesman for the South, speaking in support of states' rights and defending slavery.

John C. Calhoun was Adams's vice president, but was never close to Adams politically. In 1828, Calhoun was elected vice president again and served under Andrew Jackson.

On December 3, 1828, President Adams's defeat was confirmed. More than three times more voters cast ballots in 1828 than in 1824. Jackson gained nearly 650,000 votes to Adams's 510,000. In the electoral college Jackson overwhelmed Adams, winning 178 votes to Adams's 83. This time Jackson had a clear majority. Adams felt terribly wronged by the men who had conspired to doom his presidency. "The sun of my political life sets in the deepest gloom," he wrote in his journal.

All presidents before Adams had left office to retire to private life. For John Quincy, however, there was still a great chapter to be written.

Chapter 5

Return to the Fray

By the summer of 1830, John Quincy Adams had returned to Massachusetts. His rejection in the 1828 presidential election still stung. Then in 1829 his oldest son, George, fell or jumped from a ship and was drowned. Adams found some comfort in the routine and ordinary—rising at 5 A.M., gardening, planting trees, raising chickens, walking, swimming, and reading, including his yearly rereading of the Bible.

The black dog of depression stalked him, however, and he often despaired about the future and fretted about death. "I am suffering distress of mind," he wrote, "longing . . . to give some value to the remnant of my life." Charles Francis saw "a manifest change" in his father's spirits, noting "a kind of want of purpose which alarms me."

Adams and his wife retired to the family home, Peacefield, in Quincy, Massachusetts, where his parents had lived in their retirement.

Purpose reappeared in September 1830, when Republicans in his home district suggested John Quincy run for a seat in the U.S. House of Representatives. Louisa and Charles Francis hated the idea, worrying that a return to Washington might bring out the worst in him. They had hoped he would spend more time with his family after years of putting his political career first.

For better or worse, though, politics were John Quincy's passion and destiny. He joined the race and won a lopsided victory—1,817 votes to his opponents' combined total of 652. For the first time in his career, he had won the popular vote. "No election or appointment conferred upon me ever gave me so much pleasure," he said.

John Quincy Adams was a devoted father, but he could also be impatient with his three sons. He demanded excellence and achievement, and was often disappointed by what he viewed as their laziness. Years earlier, he had written, "I had hoped that at least one of my sons would have been ambitious to excel," he wrote in his diary. Instead, "I find them all three coming to manhood with [lazy] minds. Flinching from study whenever they can."

As the boys grew to men, John Quincy's disappointment gave way to grief. George (born 1801) became a lawyer, but drowned in 1829, a possible suicide. John (born 1803) suffered from depression and heavy drinking and died in 1834.

Charles Francis Adams as a young man. During the Civil War, he served as minister to Great Britain, a position both his father and grandfather had once occupied.

Only the youngest son, Charles Francis (born 1807), lived a full life. He was the vice-presidential candidate of the Free-Soil Party (an antislavery party) in 1848, and was elected to the U.S. House of Representatives in 1858. During the Civil War, he served as U.S. minister to Great Britain. After he retired from government service, he edited and published his father's and grandfather's important papers.

In December 1831, former president Adams took his seat in the U.S. House of Representatives. He quickly marched into the middle of the country's greatest national crisis, before or since—slavery.

Today we have a difficult time understanding how anyone could support slavery. In the early 1800s, however, most Americans—including John Quincy Adams—considered slavery a fact of life. By the time he entered the House, however, more and more Americans were questioning slavery. Especially in New England, groups who wanted to see an immediate end to slavery were swelling in number and strength. They were called *abolitionists*.

The United States was developing into two very different regions—North and South. The North had many small farmers who cultivated their own lands. Cities were growing, and more people were working in mills and factories. The South, on the other hand, relied almost entirely on farming. The richest land was occupied by large cotton plantations, where the crops were planted, tended, and harvested by African American slaves. Southern leaders and planters were convinced that giving up slavery would destroy their economy and way of life. "Our slaves are our machinery," said Representative Augustin Smith Clayton of Georgia in 1832, "and we have as good a right to profit by them as do the Northern men to profit by the machinery they employ."

Two Views on Slavery

This defense of slavery is taken from an 1822 letter (republished in 1838) from Reverend Richard Furman to the governor of South Carolina:

Sir:

[T]he right of holding slaves is clearly established in the Holy Scriptures. . . . In the Old Testament, the Israelites were directed to purchase [slaves]. . . . And it declared that the persons purchased were to be their [slaves] forever. . . .

[T]hat much cruelty has been practiced in the slave trade . . . will not be denied. But the fullest proof of these facts will not also prove that the holding of men in subjection as slaves is a moral evil and inconsistent with Christianity. . . . [H]usbands and fathers [are sometimes] tyrants. This does not prove that. . . . the husbands' right to govern and parental authority are unlawful and wicked.

Angelina E. Grimké was an antislavery activist from South Carolina. In her 1836 *Appeal to the Christian Women of the South* she argues for an end to slavery.

I lived too long in the midst of slavery, not to know what slavery is . . . and. . . . that Anti-Slavery publications have not [exaggerated] the monstrous features of slavery at all. And many a Southerner knows this as well as I do. . . .

"Thou shalt love thy neighbor as thyself." Can we love a man as we love ourselves if we do . . . what we would not wish any one to do to us? Look too, at Christ's example. . . . Can you for a moment imagine the meek, the lowly, and compassionate Savior, a *slaveholder*? do you not shudder at this thought . . . ? But why, if slavery is not sinful?

Now, as the country expanded, a new question arose. Should slavery be allowed in new states? In general, Southerners cried "yes!" while Northerners shouted "no!" Both sides knew if they won their way in a new state, the new state would support their cause in Congress. For instance, if Florida entered as a slave state, the proslavery side would get Florida's support and votes in the U.S. Congress. On the other hand, many lawmakers who had no strong beliefs about slavery were afraid that if the proslavery and antislavery sides in Congress were not in balance, the issue could tear the country—the Union—in two.

Even though Adams had not been known as a strong antislavery man when he reached the House of Representatives in 1831, he soon took up the cause as his own. While some people seek peace and harmony in their lives, others thrive on debate and controversy. During the next 16 years John Quincy blossomed in the heat of political battle, becoming the crustiest and craftiest of political warriors in the fight against slavery.

Gagging the "Massachusetts Madman" ——

In May 1836, the House passed the "Gag Rule." This rule stated that no petitions or bills relating to slavery could be introduced. This made it nearly impossible to discuss the issue. Supporters of the Gag Rule hoped it would cool tempers and

Adams became a prominent — though often unpopular — member of the House, speaking often, especially on the subject of the Gag Rule.

allow Congress to accomplish other needed business while ignoring one contro-versial subject.

Representative Adams did not want to cool things down. He never missed a chance to blast the Gag Rule, saying it violated Americans' rights to freedom of speech. Year after year the House renewed the Gag Rule, and for almost a decade John Quincy raged against it.

Adams was especially concerned about Americans' right of *petition*, guaranteed in the First Amendment of the Constitution. Citizens can propose a new law, collect signatures of people who support their position, and send the petitions to their representatives for presentation to their fellow lawmakers.

Adams received hundreds of antislavery and anti-Gag Rule petitions from citizens, but because of the Gag Rule, the petitions were tabled—set aside without discussion. If he tried to present the petitions in a speech, he was ruled out of order and was not allowed to continue. He believed he was blocked from representing the will of his *constituents* (the citizens of his district)—the very job he was elected to do.

House chambers often rang with his high, nasal voice as he matched wits in shouting matches with his opponents. "When the principle is once begun of limiting the right of petition, where would it stop?" Adams demanded to know. If Congress could gag discussion on the subject of slavery, he argued, couldn't lawmakers silence Americans on any subject at all?

Death threats arrived from proslavery Southerners, vowing to stop Adams—sometimes called "The Massachusetts Madman." A Georgian warned him, "[You] will be shot down in the street, or your damned guts will be cut out in the dark." A Virginian demanded Adams stop submitting his "abolition petitions. . . . If you do not . . . the consequence will be that the life of our once beloved

President will be no more." Another was simply a picture of Adams with a rifle ball drawn on his forehead. The threats did not frighten John Quincy one bit. In fact, his health and attitude seemed to improve as the fight became nastier.

The *Amistad* Case

In 1841, Representative Adams furthered his antislavery reputation when he agreed to argue a famous case before the U.S. Supreme Court. The case would decide the fates of kidnapped West Africans from the Spanish ship *Amistad*. Two years earlier, soon before they were to be sold as slaves in Cuba, these Africans had rebelled and captured the *Amistad*, killing the captain and cook. They ordered the remaining crew to return them to Africa. The sailors tricked the Africans, however, sailing north instead of east. The ship ran aground on the coast of Connecticut.

The U.S. court system was called on to settle the issue. Should the Africans be considered property and sent into slavery? Or were they free people, since taking Africans from Africa and selling them in North America had been declared illegal years earlier?

Now 73, John Quincy delivered a rousing defense, leading one Supreme Court justice to say about Adams's argument, "Extraordinary, I say, for its power and its bitter sarcasm." The prisoners were freed and later returned to their home in West Africa.

Adams's argument before the Supreme Court in favor of the *Amistad* captives was published and widely read. The Court ruled in the captives' favor, and they returned to their homes in West Africa.

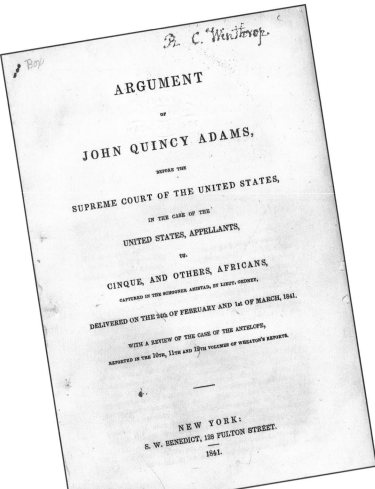

ARGUMENT

OF

JOHN QUINCY ADAMS,

BEFORE THE

SUPREME COURT OF THE UNITED STATES,

IN THE CASE OF THE

UNITED STATES, APPELLANTS,

vs.

CINQUE, AND OTHERS, AFRICANS,

CAPTURED IN THE SCHOONER AMISTAD, BY LIEUT. GEDNEY,

DELIVERED ON THE 24th OF FEBRUARY AND 1st OF MARCH, 1841.

WITH A REVIEW OF THE CASE OF THE ANTELOPE,

REPORTED IN THE 10TH, 11TH AND 12TH VOLUMES OF WHEATON'S REPORTS.

———

NEW YORK:
S. W. BENEDICT, 128 FULTON STREET.
——
1841.

A flier opposed to the slave uprising on the *Amistad* provides a sensational picture of the death of the ship's captain.

Death of Capt. Ferrer, the Captain of the Amistad, July, 1839.

Don Jose Ruiz and Don Pedro Montez, of the Island of Cuba, having purchased fifty-three slaves at Havana, recently imported from Africa, put them on board the Amistad, Capt. Ferrer, in order to transport them to Principe, another port on the Island of Cuba. After being out from Havana about four days, the African captives on board, in order to obtain their freedom, and return to Africa, armed themselves with cane knives, and rose upon the Captain and crew of the vessel. Capt. Ferrer and the cook of the vessel were killed; two of the crew escaped; Ruiz and Montez were made prisoners.

Censure and Success

In January 1842, Adams forced his opponents in Congress into a mistake. He presented a petition from his constituents that called for New England states to leave the Union. The petition argued that it was unfair that free states had to pay taxes to support slavery and protect southern states from slave uprisings. The House exploded in anger, and Adams's enemies called him a traitor for proposing to break up the United States. They voted to *censure* (condemn) him for the act.

New Developments in Adams's Time

Adams saw many life-changing developments in his later years. Here are some examples:

1830 Steam Locomotive: The first short railroads begin replacing horses and carriages. (John Quincy personally experienced a train wreck in 1833.)

1835 Revolver: Samuel Colt develops one of the first guns able to fire several shots without reloading.

1842 Baseball: Young men in New York City begin playing a new game called "base ball."

1843 Sewing Machine: Elias Howe builds a machine to replace handheld needle and thread.

1843 Photography: Adams becomes the first U.S. president to sit for a portrait captured on daguerreotype, an early form of the photograph. This technique, invented in France, was first used in the United States in 1839.

1844 Telegraph: Samuel F. B. Morse sends the first long-distance electrical message—"What hath God wrought!"—from Washington, D.C., to Baltimore, Maryland.

☆ ☆ ☆

By censuring him, they had played right into his hands. By law, he now had the right to speak freely to defend himself. He mercilessly ripped into slavery, the Gag Rule, and his proslavery enemies. "If before I get through," he said, "every slaveholder, slave trader and slave breeder on this floor does not get materials for bitter reflection, it shall be no fault of mine."

Adams escaped punishment for his bold stunt, and even earned the respect of his opponents. The publicity his arguments received informed many Americans not just about the horrors of slavery but about the dangers of the Gag Rule. Finally, in 1844, Adams got the triumph he had fought eight angry years to win. On December 3, House members voted to end the Gag Rule. On hearing the final tally, John Quincy cried out, "Blessed, forever, blessed be the name of God!"

Death at His Post

Early in 1845, Congress voted to *annex* (take control of) Texas, land that was also claimed by Mexico. This move set the stage for war with Mexico. It was also a setback for the antislavery movement, since there was little question that Texas would be admitted to the Union as a slave state. Adams opposed the annexation. In 1846, when President James K. Polk pushed for a declaration of war against

Pioneer photographer Mathew Brady made this portrait of the aged John Quincy Adams.

Fast Facts

MEXICAN-AMERICAN WAR

Who: The United States against Mexico.

When: May 1846 through October 1847. (Peace treaty signed in February 1848.)

Why: Simmering tensions and the 1845 U.S. annexation of Texas sparked fighting, then a U.S. landgrab. With the signing of the Treaty of Guadalupe Hidalgo in 1848, the U.S. gained the rest of modern-day Texas; all of California, Utah, and Nevada; and most of Arizona and New Mexico.

Result: Mexico ceded the vast Texas territory to the United States. It included all or most of present-day Texas, New Mexico, Colorado, Arizona, Utah, Nevada, and California.

Mexico, Adams was one of only 14 representatives to vote no, against 174 who were in favor.

Adams's stand on the Mexican War was unpopular, yet to many in the northern states he had become a hero. To his surprise, he finally had a popular following. Wherever he traveled in the North, he was received enthusiastically. "Crowds of people were assembled [along the railroad track], received me with three cheers, and manifested a desire to see and hear me," he noted with pleasure. As much of a grump as John Quincy could be, he still appreciated public praise and affection.

By 1845, however, his health was failing. He suffered a small stroke, then a crippling one in late 1847. Still, he battled back and returned to his desk in the House. On February 21, 1848, he was at that desk when he collapsed. He was carried to an office, where he died two days later. "A Sage has fallen at his Post,"

John Quincy Adams collapsed at his desk in the House of Representatives in February 1848 and died two days later.

read one funeral notice. After 53 years in service to his country, John Quincy Adams—son of patriots and tireless defender of the rights and freedoms of the young United States—could not have asked for a better death.

Chapter 6

A Founder of American Foreign Policy

John Quincy Adams believed his presidency was a failure, and most historians agree. As the nation's sixth president, he tried to lead the United States where most citizens were not ready to go. His inflexible leadership and moody personality made him difficult to work with and earned him many enemies. Politically weak after winning the controversial 1824 election, John Quincy watched as his presidential hopes and plans were easily sabotaged.

Still, John Quincy Adams was one of the most important American diplomats and public officials during the first half of the 1800s. He possessed the intelligence, principles, and courage to look beyond what was politically popular or convenient. He proved himself a brave statesman, fighting for what he felt was moral and right in the face of heavy criticism, risking his own career, his reputation—

even his life. He left a legacy that can still be felt today in the United States and around the globe.

Adams was perhaps the most influential diplomat the United States has ever produced. When he began his career, the United States of America was like a new sixth-grader in middle school, trying to figure out how to get along with older, stronger kids. As the U.S. minister to the Netherlands, Prussia, Russia, and Great Britain, John Quincy helped his young country carve out its place in the community of nations. He negotiated some of the most important treaties in early U.S. history—including the Treaty of Ghent with Great Britain ending the War of 1812, and the Transcontinental Treaty of 1819 with Spain, gaining the territory of Florida for the United States.

As a minister, and later as secretary of state for eight years, Adams helped set the style for the country's budding foreign policy. His contributions fell into three main categories: (1) expanding the territory of the United States; (2) avoiding involvement in Europe's troubles; and (3) protecting the Americas from foreign interference.

Expanding the United States

John Quincy was one of the first American leaders to believe that the United States would one day stretch from the Atlantic to the Pacific Oceans. In 1811, he wrote to his father, "The whole continent of North America appears to be destined . . . to be peopled by one nation, speaking one language, professing one general system of religious and political principles."

His words and actions began to change this belief into reality. John Quincy's negotiations with Great Britain and Spain added Florida and the Pacific Northwest to the country's territories. In his lifetime, he saw his country grow from 13 to 29 states along borders he helped create.

Late in his life "manifest destiny" became a rallying cry for many westward-looking Americans. As editor John L. O'Sullivan wrote in 1845, "[O]ur manifest destiny [is] to overspread the continent allotted by Providence for the development of our yearly multiplying millions."

The idea fueled enthusiasm for the Mexican-American War, which added the largest new territory to the United States since the Louisiana Purchase in 1803. Even though Adams opposed the war, the new territory helped fulfill his earlier dreams. The Oregon Treaty of 1846 brought more land, dividing the original Oregon Territory which the United States and Britain occupied together. The U.S. share included the present-day states of Washington, Oregon, Idaho, and parts of Montana and Wyoming. By the time Adams died, nearly all the land of the United States today, except for Alaska and Hawaii, had been acquired.

Avoiding Foreign Entanglements ──────────

Adams became expert at working with European powers as a diplomat, but he was determined to keep the United States from getting dragged into their troubles and spats. When France sought support in its wars with Great Britain, he argued against taking sides. Likewise, when Great Britain wanted the United States as a partner to block Spain's interference in South America, Secretary of State Adams refused.

He argued that if the United States became too closely linked to another country, it could be forced to fight in wars it did not start, and "She would be no longer the ruler of her own spirit." This strict policy of avoiding alliances lasted until 1917, when the United States entered World War I in support of its allies in Europe. In many cases, Americans still prefer to "go it alone" when dealing with international crises.

Protecting the Americas ──────────────

Adams was a major contributor to the Monroe Doctrine, developed under President James Monroe. This policy warned world powers not to intervene in the affairs of countries in North and South America, and it was intended to prevent European nations from establishing new colonies or stirring up trouble in the U.S. backyard. This old doctrine still influences U.S. policies today.

While he wrote these rules for international relations, Adams also pushed and prodded other countries to respect U.S. shipping rights and rights to do business. Taken all together, John Quincy Adams's foreign policy efforts safeguarded the United States from outside dangers while the young country grew, matured, and gathered strength.

National Vision

On the home front, Adams was a devoted nationalist. While many Americans of his time still felt more connected to their home states than to their country, he urged them to bond together and act together as one nation. Similarly, he urged fellow politicians to put their country ahead of their political party, working together to develop the country as a whole. "The object nearest to my heart [is] to bring the whole people of the Union to harmonize together," he wrote.

Adams envisioned the federal government building roads and canals to move people and goods across the country. He wanted to create a national university, a U.S. naval academy, and national centers for scientific research and exploration. To his great disappointment, many of his ideas were rejected. If he had lived a hundred years later, he would have seen most Americans and states embrace his belief in cooperation and national improvement.

The Smithsonian Institution

As president, Adams saw his hopes dashed for building national institutions for education and research. Strangely, it was a British man, James Smithson, who gave John Quincy the chance to see a small part of that dream come true.

In 1835, Smithson left about $500,000 to the United States in his will, "for the increase . . . of knowledge among men." Adams was named chairman of the committee to decide what to do with these funds. For the next ten years, he protected the money from "hungry and worthless political jackals" who wanted to use the gift for personal projects. Finally in 1846, Congress created the Smithsonian Institution.

At first, the Smithsonian housed a museum, laboratory, library, and art gallery in a single building. Today it has grown into the world's largest museum and research complex, including 15 museums and the National Zoo—thanks in part to John Quincy Adams.

An early photograph of the "castle" housing the Smithsonian Institution, which Adams helped guide through its earliest days. Today the building is the information center for the Smithsonian's many museums and offices in Washington.

Adams saw national teamwork not only as an efficient way to make improvements but also as a way to protect the Union. As different states and different regions competed with one another, he feared that growing disagreements would endanger the country's unity.

The gravest disagreement, of course, was between North and South over issues related to slavery. John Quincy warned that the quarrel would sooner or later split up the country. Thirteen years after his death, his prediction proved too true, when southern states voted to create their own country and tensions exploded in the U.S. Civil War (1861–1865). More Americans died during those four years of fighting than in any war before or since.

The North's victory reunited the states into one country and also brought an end to slavery. The Civil War also forged a stronger federal government and a growing sense of national identity among Americans. These results would have pleased John Quincy Adams, but he would have been horrified by their cost in lives and suffering.

A Battler for Human Rights ——————————

Adams was also ahead of his time in recognizing the rights and humanity of Native Americans and African Americans. Like his parents John and Abigail,

Adams had a strong sense of right and wrong, and these beliefs were even stronger than his love of the United States. He said he would never wish "of heaven success, even for my country, in a cause where she would be in the wrong." In their treatment of slaves and Native Americans, he felt his country was terribly wrong.

Most white Americans of John Quincy's time viewed Native Americans, or Indians, as savages. And as white settlers pushed west, many felt it was their right—even their duty—to take the land from America's native peoples. As president, Adams tried to protect the Creek and other tribes from unfair treatment, but it was a battle he could not win. Public opinion was fiercely against him as state and federal officials swindled and killed American Indians for their land.

Later in his life, John Quincy wrote, "We [the United States] have done more harm to the Indians since our Revolution than had ever been done to them by the French and English nations before. . . . These are crying sins for which we are answerable before a higher jurisdiction." In other words, he believed Americans would have to answer to God for their poor treatment and crimes against American Indian tribes.

On the issue of slavery, Adams walked a fine line in seeking an end to slavery in the United States. There was no question that he believed "slavery to be a sin before the sight of God" and "That nature's God commands the slave to rise, / And on the oppressor's head to break the chain." He backed up his words with action, as when he defended the African prisoners from the *Amistad*.

He also worried that extreme antislavery groups—the abolitionists— sometimes acted too aggressively and "in zeal they kindle the opposition against themselves into a flame." Both pro- and antislavery forces, he feared, were willing to wreck the country for their beliefs and interests.

His hope was that slavery could be phased out while avoiding war and preserving the Union of states. In 1839, he proposed that "after the 4th day of July, 1842 . . . every child born within the United States . . . shall be born free." His proposal also suggested that slavery be banned in all new states. But slavery proved too hot an issue to be resolved by thoughtful planning. Its end came only with the crisis and violence of the Civil War.

Late in his life, Adams also developed a reputation as a defender of women's rights, long before women had even the right to vote. When a Maryland representative attacked a petition because it was signed by women, John Quincy replied, "Are women to have no opinions or actions on subjects relating to the general welfare?" He then went on to name great women in world history, ending the list with "the ladies of our own Revolution." In reality, Adams

Women's Roles in Early America

In the early 1800s, the role of women in society was limited to the home. They were expected to marry, obey their husbands, bear and raise children, and keep house. Many gave birth to eight or more children, and many more died of complications during pregnancy and childbirth. Keeping a house in the days before laborsaving devices required much hard work—carrying water, cooking over an open fire, washing, and tending gardens. For all their hard work, women usually could not attend school, and were restricted from owning or inheriting property and from operating their own businesses. Voting was restricted to men. In wealthier families, a girl might receive some education at home, learning to read, write, and do arithmetic. She might also receive lessons in music and dancing. Still, her ambitions were limited to marriage, motherhood, and running a household.

★★★

still held the common view that men should manage the political life of the country. Yet his defense of women's opinions won him the admiration of many women, some of whom expressed their thanks by sending him knitted socks, scarves, and hand warmers.

For all his faults, John Quincy Adams was a brave and hardworking statesman who stubbornly battled for what he felt was right. He had little success

ALTERI · SECULO

A · Ω

Near this Place
Reposes all that could die of
JOHN QUINCY ADAMS,
Son of John and Abigail [Smith] Adams,
Sixth President of the United States,
Born 11 July, 1767,
Amidst the Storms of civil Commotion
He nursed the Vigor
Which nerves a Statesman and a Patriot,
And the Faith
Which inspires a Christian.
For more than half a Century,
Whenever his Country called for his Labors,
In either Hemisphere or in any Capacity,
He never spared them in her Cause.
On the twenty-fourth of December, 1814,
He signed the second Treaty with Great Britain,
Which restored Peace within her Borders.
On the twenty-third of February, 1848,
He closed sixteen years of eloquent Defence
Of the Lessons of his Youth,
By dying at his Post
In her great national Council.

A Son, worthy of his Father,
A Citizen, shedding glory on his Country,
A Scholar, ambitious to advance Mankind,
This Christian sought to walk humbly
In the Sight of his God.

Beside him lies
His Partner for fifty Years,
LOUISA CATHERINE,
Daughter of Joshua and Catherine [Nuth] Johnson,
Born, 12 February, 1775,
Married, 26 July, 1797,
Deceased, 15 May, 1852,
Aged 77.
Living through many Vicissitudes, and
Under high Responsibilities,
As a Daughter, Wife and Mother,
She proved equal to all.
Dying, she left to her Family and her Sex
The blessed Remembrance
Of a 'Woman that feareth the Lord'.

"HEREIN IS THAT SAYING TRUE, ONE SOWETH AND ANOTHER REAPETH, I SENT YOU TO REAP THAT WHEREON
YE BESTOWED NO LABOR, OTHER MEN LABORED, AND YE ARE ENTERED INTO THEIR LABORS."

This memorial to John Quincy and Louisa Adams stands in the churchyard of the United First Parish Church in Quincy, Massachusetts. The churchyard is now part of the Adams National Historical Park.

as president, but in his long career both before and after the presidency, he contributed much to the security and growth of the nation. He was a champion of the American ideals of freedom and fairness, and he was a hopeful visionary of what the United States and its people could and would become.

Fast Facts John Quincy Adams

Birth:	July 11, 1767
Birthplace:	Braintree (now Quincy), Massachusetts
Parents:	John and Abigail Smith Adams
Brothers & Sisters:	Abigail "Nabby" Adams Smith (1765–1813)
	Susanna Adams (1768–1770)
	Charles Adams (1770–1800)
	Thomas Boylston Adams (1772–1832)
Education:	Graduated Harvard College, 1787
	Studied law privately
Occupation:	Lawyer, diplomat
Marriage:	To Louisa Catherine Johnson, July 26, 1797, in London, England
Children:	George (1801–1829)
	John Jr. (1803–1834)
	Charles Francis (1807–1886)
	Louisa Catherine (1811–1812)
Political Parties	Federalist; Democratic-Republican
Political Offices:	1794 Minister to the Netherlands
	1797–01 Minister to Prussia
	1803–08 United States Senator from Massachusetts
	1809–11 Minister to Russia
	1814 Peace Commissioner at Treaty of Ghent
	1815–17 Minister to Great Britain
	1817–25 Secretary of State under President Monroe
	1825–29 Sixth President of the United States
	1831–48 Member, U.S. House of Representatives
His Vice President:	John C. Calhoun
Major Actions as President:	Supported new commercial treaties with many European countries
	Sought (but failed) to protect Native Americans' land in Georgia
	Proposed many programs supporting learning and research
Firsts:	Son of a president to be elected president himself
	To serve in elective office after leaving the presidency
Death:	February 23, 1848
Age at Death:	80 years
Burial Place:	United First Parish Church, Quincy, Massachusetts

Fast Facts

Louisa Catherine Johnson Adams

Birth:	February 12, 1775
Birthplace:	London, England
Parents:	Joshua and Carolyn Nuth Johnson
Education:	Home taught; was an accomplished musician and a poet
Marriage:	To John Quincy Adams, July 26, 1797, in London
Children:	*See* list under John Quincy Adams at left
Firsts:	First foreign-born wife to serve as first lady
Death:	May 15, 1852
Age at Death:	77 years
Burial Place:	United First Parish Church, Quincy, Massachusetts

Timeline

1767	1776	1778	1782	1785
Born on July 11.	United States declares independence from Great Britain.	Accompanies father to France.	Goes to Russia as secretary and interpreter for U.S. official Francis Dana.	Returns to the United States.

1807	1809	1812	1814	1815
Third son, Charles Francis, born.	Appointed minister to Russia by President Madison.	Infant daughter, Louisa Catherine, dies.	Heads U.S. team that negotiates the Treaty of Ghent, ending U.S.-British War of 1812.	Appointed minister to Great Britain.

1827	1828	1830	1835	1836
Blocked when he tried to protect Creek Indian lands in Georgia.	Runs for reelection, is defeated by Andrew Jackson.	Elected to U.S. House of Representatives.	Appointed chairman of committee that will establish the Smithsonian Institution.	House passes "Gag Rule" banning anti-slavery discussion and petitions.

1787	1794	1797	1801	1803
Graduates from Harvard second in his class.	Appointed minister to the Netherlands by President Washington.	Father, John Adams, becomes second U.S. president. John Quincy appointed minister to Prussia. Marries Louisa Catherine Johnson.	Recalled from Prussia. First son, George Washington Adams, born.	Elected to U.S. Senate. Second son, John Adams II, born.

1817	1819	1823	1824	1825
Appointed secretary of state by President Monroe.	Signs Transcontinental Treaty with Spain turning Florida over to the United States.	Monroe Doctrine announced.	Runs for president. No candidate receives a majority of electoral votes.	Is elected by U.S. House of Representatives. Accused of a "corrupt bargain" to win election over Andrew Jackson.

1841	1844	1845	1846	1848
Successfully defends *Amistad* African captives before U.S. Supreme Court.	After an 8-year fight, Adams helps defeat the Gag Rule.	Efforts to prevent annexation of Texas defeated.	Votes against declaration of war with Mexico.	Collapses at his desk in the House and dies on February 23.

Glossary

abolitionists: members of a movement demanding the immediate end (abolition) of slavery

annex: to take control or ownership of a region

British Parliament: lawmaking body in Great Britain

cede: to give territory to another country

censure: to officially criticize or condemn

colony: territory settled and controlled by a distant country

constituents: citizens represented by an elected official (such as a congressman or senator)

diplomacy: discussions between countries to solve problems peacefully

embargo: ban, usually relating to business trading

exports: goods sold to another country

federal government: national or central government

foreign policy: a plan for dealing with other countries

import: to bring goods from another country

impress: in naval history, to capture a foreign seaman and force him to serve on an enemy ship against his will

majority: in a vote, more than half of the votes cast; a majority of 24 votes is 13 or more

negotiate: to discuss a dispute in order to reach an agreement

petition: a statement, often with many signatures, presented to a government proposing a new law or urging support for a position

presidential administration: a group that includes the president and president's advisers

tariff: a tax on imports and/or exports

treaty: an official agreement between countries

veto: in U.S. government, a president's refusal to sign into law a bill passed by Congress; Congress can **override** a president's veto by passing the bill by two-thirds majorities in the House and the Senate

Further Reading

Joseph, Paul. *John Quincy Adams*. Edina, MN: Abdo Publishing Co., 1999.

Kent, Zachary. *John Quincy Adams: Sixth President of the United States*. Chicago: Children's Press, 1987.

Kroll, Stephen. *John Quincy Adams: Letters from a Southern Planter's Son*. New York: Winslow Press, 2001.

Walker, Jane C. *John Quincy Adams*. Berkeley Heights, NJ: Enslow, 2000.

MORE ADVANCED READING

Adams, John Quincy. *The Diary of John Quincy Adams 1794–1845*. New York: Longmans, Green and Co., 1928.

Bemis, Samuel Flagg. *John Quincy Adams and the Foundations of American Foreign Policy*. New York: Alfred A. Knopf, 1949.

East, Robert A. *John Quincy Adams: The Critical Years*. New York: Bookman Associates, Inc., 1962.

Grimké, Angelina E. *Appeal to the Christian Women of the South*. New York: New York Anti-Slavery Society, 1836.

Hecht, Marie B. *John Quincy Adams*. New York: Macmillan Company, 1972.

Nagel, Paul C. *John Quincy Adams*. New York: Alfred A. Knopf, 1997.

Russell, Greg. *John Quincy Adams and the Public Virtues of Diplomacy*. Columbia, MO: University of Missouri Press, 1995.

Shepherd, Jack. *The Adams Chronicles*. Boston: Little, Brown & Company, 1975.

———. *Cannibals of the Heart: A Personal Biography of Louisa Catherine and John Quincy Adams*. New York: McGraw-Hill, 1980.

Places to Visit

Adams National Historical Site

135 Adams Street

Quincy, MA

(617) 770-1175

http://www.nps.gov/adam/

Birthplace, presidential library, and family crypt for John Adams, John Quincy Adams, and their wives.

Smithsonian Institution

National Mall

Washington, D.C.

Visit the collection of Smithsonian museums that John Quincy Adams helped to establish. For more information,

Smithsonian Information

P.O. Box 37012

SI Building, Room 153, MRC010

Washington, D.C. 20013-7012

(202) 257-2700

http://www.si.edu/

Online Sites of Interest

★**American Presidents**

http://www.americanpresident.org/kotrain/courses/JQA

Provides facts about John Quincy Adams and much additional information on his childhood, political career, presidency, and retirement.

★**Internet Public Library, Presidents of the United States (IPL POTUS)**

http://www.ipl.org/ref/POTUS/jqadams.html

Excellent resource for personal, political, and historical information about John Quincy Adams. It includes links to other useful Web sites.

★**The White House**

http://www.whitehouse.gov/history/presidents/ja6.html

Provides a brief biography of John Quincy Adams. The site also provides information on the current president, biographies of other presidents, and information on timely topics of interest.

★**The Adams Papers**

Massachusetts Historical Society

http://www.masshist.org/adams.html

For additional online sites, *see* "Places to Visit."

Table of Presidents

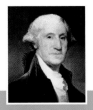   

	1. George Washington	**2. John Adams**	**3. Thomas Jefferson**	**4. James Madison**
Took office	Apr 30 1789	Mar 4 1797	Mar 4 1801	Mar 4 1809
Left office	Mar 3 1797	Mar 3 1801	Mar 3 1809	Mar 3 1817
Birthplace	Westmoreland Co, VA	Braintree, MA	Shadwell, VA	Port Conway, VA
Birth date	Feb 22 1732	Oct 20 1735	Apr 13 1743	Mar 16 1751
Death date	Dec 14 1799	July 4 1826	July 4 1826	June 28 1836

  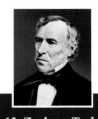

	9. William H. Harrison	**10. John Tyler**	**11. James K. Polk**	**12. Zachary Taylor**
Took office	Mar 4 1841	Apr 6 1841	Mar 4 1845	Mar 5 1849
Left office	**Apr 4 1841•**	Mar 3 1845	Mar 3 1849	**July 9 1850•**
Birthplace	Berkeley, VA	Greenway, VA	Mecklenburg Co, NC	Barboursville, VA
Birth date	Feb 9 1773	Mar 29 1790	Nov 2 1795	Nov 24 1784
Death date	Apr 4 1841	Jan 18 1862	June 15 1849	July 9 1850

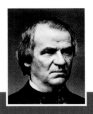    

	17. Andrew Johnson	**18. Ulysses S. Grant**	**19. Rutherford B. Hayes**	**20. James A. Garfield**
Took office	Apr 15 1865	Mar 4 1869	Mar 4 1877	Mar 4 1881
Left office	Mar 3 1869	Mar 3 1877	Mar 3 1881	**Sept 19 1881•**
Birthplace	Raleigh, NC	Point Pleasant, OH	Delaware, OH	Orange, OH
Birth date	Dec 29 1808	Apr 27 1822	Oct 4 1822	Nov 19 1831
Death date	July 31 1875	July 23 1885	Jan 17 1893	Sept 19 1881

5. James Monroe

Mar 4 1817

Mar 3 1825

Westmoreland Co, VA

Apr 28 1758

July 4 1831

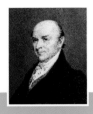

6. John Quincy Adams

Mar 4 1825

Mar 3 1829

Braintree, MA

July 11 1767

Feb 23 1848

7. Andrew Jackson

Mar 4 1829

Mar 3 1837

The Waxhaws, SC

Mar 15 1767

June 8 1845

8. Martin Van Buren

Mar 4 1837

Mar 3 1841

Kinderhook, NY

Dec 5 1782

July 24 1862

13. Millard Fillmore

July 9 1850

Mar 3 1853

Locke Township, NY

Jan 7 1800

Mar 8 1874

14. Franklin Pierce

Mar 4 1853

Mar 3 1857

Hillsborough, NH

Nov 23 1804

Oct 8 1869

15. James Buchanan

Mar 4 1857

Mar 3 1861

Cove Gap, PA

Apr 23 1791

June 1 1868

16. Abraham Lincoln

Mar 4 1861

Apr 15 1865•

Hardin Co, KY

Feb 12 1809

Apr 15 1865

21. Chester A. Arthur

Sept 19 1881

Mar 3 1885

Fairfield, VT

Oct 5 1830

Nov 18 1886

22. Grover Cleveland

Mar 4 1885

Mar 3 1889

Caldwell, NJ

Mar 18 1837

June 24 1908

23. Benjamin Harrison

Mar 4 1889

Mar 3 1893

North Bend, OH

Aug 20 1833

Mar 13 1901

24. Grover Cleveland

Mar 4 1893

Mar 3 1897

Caldwell, NJ

Mar 18 1837

June 24 1908

   ...

	25. William McKinley	**26. Theodore Roosevelt**	**27. William H. Taft**	**28. Woodrow Wilson**
Took office	Mar 4 1897	Sept 14 1901	Mar 4 1909	Mar 4 1913
Left office	**Sept 14 1901•**	Mar 3 1909	Mar 3 1913	Mar 3 1921
Birthplace	Niles, OH	New York, NY	Cincinnati, OH	Staunton, VA
Birth date	Jan 29 1843	Oct 27 1858	Sept 15 1857	Dec 28 1856
Death date	Sept 14 1901	Jan 6 1919	Mar 8 1930	Feb 3 1924

	33. Harry S. Truman	**34. Dwight D. Eisenhower**	**35. John F. Kennedy**	**36. Lyndon B. Johnson**
Took office	Apr 12 1945	Jan 20 1953	Jan 20 1961	Nov 22 1963
Left office	Jan 20 1953	Jan 20 1961	**Nov 22 1963•**	Jan 20 1969
Birthplace	Lamar, MO	Denison, TX	Brookline, MA	Johnson City, TX
Birth date	May 8 1884	Oct 14 1890	May 29 1917	Aug 27 1908
Death date	Dec 26 1972	Mar 28 1969	Nov 22 1963	Jan 22 1973

	41. George Bush	**42. Bill Clinton**	**43. George W. Bush**
Took office	Jan 20 1989	Jan 20 1993	Jan 20 2001
Left office	Jan 20 1993	Jan 20 2001	—
Birthplace	Milton, MA	Hope, AR	New Haven, CT
Birth date	June 12 1924	Aug 19 1946	July 6 1946
Death date	—	—	—

29. Warren G. Harding	30. Calvin Coolidge	31. Herbert Hoover	32. Franklin D. Roosevelt
Mar 4 1921	Aug 2 1923	Mar 4 1929	Mar 4 1933
Aug 2 1923•	Mar 3 1929	Mar 3 1933	**Apr 12 1945**•
Blooming Grove, OH	Plymouth, VT	West Branch, IA	Hyde Park, NY
Nov 21 1865	July 4 1872	Aug 10 1874	Jan 30 1882
Aug 2 1923	Jan 5 1933	Oct 20 1964	Apr 12 1945

37. Richard M. Nixon	38. Gerald R. Ford	39. Jimmy Carter	40. Ronald Reagan
Jan 20 1969	Aug 9 1974	Jan 20 1977	Jan 20 1981
Aug 9 1974★	Jan 20 1977	Jan 20 1981	Jan 20 1989
Yorba Linda, CA	Omaha, NE	Plains, GA	Tampico, IL
Jan 9 1913	July 14 1913	Oct 1 1924	Feb 11 1911
Apr 22 1994	—	—	—

• Indicates the president died while in office.

★ Richard Nixon resigned before his term expired.

Index

Page numbers in *italics* indicate illustrations

Monroe, James, 32, 41, 45
Monroe Doctrine, 45, *46*, 86–87

Napoleon I, Emperor of the French, 32, 37
nationalism, 87, 89
Native Americans, 37, 56–57, 89, 90
nepotism, 26
Netherlands, 17, 25–26
neutrality, 86
New Orleans, Louisiana, 32
"No taxation without representation!", 11
Non-Importation Act, 30
North, the (region of the United States), 70, 72

Oregon Territory, 43, 85
O'Sullivan, John L., 85

Paris, Treaty of (1783), 19
Parsons, Theophilus, 23
Peacefield (home of John Quincy Adams), *68*
petition, right of, 74
plantations, 70
Polk, James K., 78
Prussia, 28

Revolutionary War. *See* American Revolution
Russia, 17, 35–37

St. Petersburg, Russia, 35–36, *36*
Seminole (Native Americans), 43–44
Senate, United States, 29–30, 34
ship travel, slowness of, 15

slavery, 70–78, 89, 90–91
Smithson, James, 88
Smithsonian Institution, 88, *88*
South, the (region of the United States), 62, 70, 72
Spain, territorial issues with, 43–45, 85
"Star-Spangled Banner, The," 39
states during Adams's presidency, map of, 60
states' rights, 56–57

Tariff of Abominations, 62
tariffs, 62
taxation, 10–11, 62
territorial expansion of the United States, 84–85
Texas, 78
Transcontinental Treaty, 44–45, 84
travel, slowness of, 15
Troup, George, 56

War of 1812, 37, 39
    fast facts, 39
War of Independence. *See* American Revolution
Washington, D.C., British attack on, 37
Washington, George, 11, 19, 25, 26, 28
westward movement, 84–85
White House, 63
women's rights, 91–92
women's role in early America, 92

Yorktown, Battle of, 19

About the Author

John Quincy Adams kept a diary for 68 years, from his earliest career until his death. The author, Sean McCollum, spent hour after hour reading these volumes. In John Quincy's own words, these diaries offer fascinating glimpses into his life, personality, and times.

Sean has authored six books and hundreds of magazine articles. He has traveled to more than 40 countries, but lives in the mountains near Boulder, Colorado, where he's surrounded by deer, foxes, woodpeckers, and aspen trees.